HISTORY'S FORGOTTEN WAR STORIES

by Janet Slingerland

www.12StoryLibrary.com

Copyright © 2019 by 12-Story Library, Mankato, MN 56003. All rights reserved. No part of this book may be reproduced or utilized in any form or by any means without written permission from the publisher.

12-Story Library is an imprint of Bookstaves.

Photographs ©: PD, cover, 1; PD, 4; Zenit/CC3.0, 5; PD, 6; Lat34North/PD, 7; Edward Clifton Wharton/PD, 8; PD, 9; A. H. Ritchie/Library of Congress, 10; John Schanlaub/CC4.0, 11; Internet Archive Book Images/CC, 11; Library of Congress, 12; US National Library of Medicine/PD, 13; PD, 14; US Department of Defense, 15; US Central Intelligence Agency, 16; CIA People/PD, 17; Everett Collection Inc/Alamy Stock Photo, 18; Tootsie Roll/PD, 19; Evan-Amos/CC3.0, 19; US Army, 20; West Point/US Army, 21; 1st Class Brien Aho/US Navy, 22; US Navy, 23; PH1 Elliott/US Department of Defense, 24; Associated Press, 25; US Department of Defense, 26; Mel Evans/Associated Press, 27; US GOVT/US Army, 28; US Navy, 29

ISBN
978-1-63235-593-5 (hardcover)
978-1-63235-647-5 (paperback)
978-1-63235-706-9 (ebook)

Library of Congress Control Number: 2018947113

Printed in the United States of America
Mankato, MN
July 2018

About the Cover
An undated image of Choctaw Indians in training for World War I.

Access free, up-to-date content on this topic plus a full digital version of this book. Scan the QR code on page 31 or use your school's login at 12StoryLibrary.com.

Table of Contents

The Turtle Attacks 4

Nancy Hart Fights the British 6

American Soldiers March to a Slave's Drum 8

Anson Stager Stumps the Confederates 10

Dr. Anita McGee Helps Nurses Join the Army 12

Choctaw Soldiers Turn the Tables in World War I 14

The "Limping Lady" Takes on the Nazis 16

Tootsie Rolls Save Marines in Korean War 18

Lucki Allen Paves the Way for Women Interrogators 20

Marine Mammals Perform Important Tasks in Wartime 22

First American Woman Leads Troops in Combat 24

Soldiers Use Silly String to Detect Trip Wires in Iraq 26

Fact Sheet 28

Glossary 30

For More Information 31

Index 32

About the Author 32

The Turtle Attacks

David Bushnell started Yale College in 1771. While there, he figured out how to explode gunpowder underwater. During his senior year, the American Revolution began. Yale closed early. Bushnell returned home to his Connecticut farm. He worked on a way to deliver his underwater mine.

Bushnell designed a submarine. It moved forwards and backwards. It could dive under a ship and attach the mine. It could then return to the surface. Bushnell's brother Ezra helped construct this vessel. They made it from oak planks and iron rings. The boat looked like two turtle shells put together. The Bushnells called it the Turtle.

The Turtle was powered by a treadle and a hand crank. The pilot got air from two snorkels. These closed when the boat was underwater. Weights on the Turtle's bottom kept it upright. The boat submerged by taking on

In 1775, the Turtle failed at fastening mines to ships.

A reproduction of the Turtle.

water. It surfaced by pumping the water out.

A man named Ezra Lee piloted the Turtle's first mission. On September 7, 1776, he pedaled into New York Harbor. After two and half hours, he reached the British Admiral Howe's flagship. He submerged the Turtle. Under the ship, Lee tried to attach the mine. The screw wouldn't go in.

Lee was out of time. The Turtle returned to the surface. British guards gave chase. Lee let the mine go. It exploded, scaring off his pursuers.

The Turtle tried and failed twice more. On October 9, 1776, the Turtle was moving to a new port. The British attacked. David Bushnell and Ezra Lee survived. The Turtle did not.

150
Pounds of gunpowder (68 kg) in the underwater mine.

- David Bushnell discovered how to explode gunpowder underwater.
- He invented a submarine to deliver this mine.
- The first submarine attack happened during the Revolutionary War.

Nancy Hart Fights the British

Nancy Morgan Hart stood six feet (1.8 m) tall. She was muscular and had fiery red hair. The Cherokee called her "Wahatche." This means "War Woman."

In the 1770s, the Hart family moved to the Georgia frontier. When the American Revolution started, Nancy's husband joined the militia. Nancy protected their property and children. Nancy found other ways to help, too. She dressed like a man and acted feebleminded. She roamed British camps, collecting information. She passed this information to the Patriots.

Hart faced danger at home. Tories demanded that settlers sign an oath of allegiance to the British king. One of the Harts' neighbors refused. He

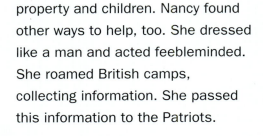

1735
Year Nancy Morgan is believed to have been born.

- The Revolutionary War reached Nancy Morgan Hart on the Georgia frontier.
- She dressed as a man to spy on British soldiers.
- Nancy and her daughter captured a group of British soldiers.

was shot dead in front of his family. The group of five or six Tories then went to the Harts' cabin. Nancy and her 12-year-old daughter, Sukey, were there alone.

The Tories demanded food. The Harts fed them and gave them whiskey. The Tories relaxed. They propped their muskets up in a corner. Nancy passed several muskets to Sukey through a hole in the wall. One soldier noticed and jumped up to stop her. Nancy shot and killed him. She wounded another. She held the remaining men hostage until her husband and neighbors arrived. After much debate, the Patriots hanged the Tories from a nearby tree.

FACT OR FICTION?

Many variations of Nancy's encounter with the Tories have been told. The story became a local legend. No one knows for sure what happened that day. In 1912, six skeletons were found near the Hart homestead. This confirmed that some version of the story was true.

American Soldiers March to a Slave's Drum

Jordan Noble was born in Georgia around 1800. He and his mother were slaves. During the war of 1812, they were sold to an officer in the New Orleans 7th Regiment. Jordan took Lt. Noble's name. He also learned to drum.

American General Andrew Jackson led an attack on December 23, 1814. The 7th Regiment marched into battle. Young Jordan Noble kept the beat. The fog was thick that night. Noble's steady beat helped the soldiers keep their bearings. It led them to victory.

Andrew Jackson's army fought the British again on January 8, 1815. Again, Noble's steady beat kept the Americans going. The Americans won the Battle of New Orleans, the last battle of the war.

Drummers were critical to the army. Every morning, they woke the soldiers with reveille. They called soldiers to roll call and officers to meetings. They set the tempo and direction of marches. On the battlefield, they issued commands to the soldiers. Each command had a different rhythmic beat.

Jordan Noble in 1885.

During downtime, drummers helped morale. Along with military bands, they entertained the troops. On the battlefield, the drum beat rallied the troops and gave them energy. When the battle ended, the drummers honored the fallen with a funeral march.

Jordan gained his freedom in 1837. He served in three other wars, including the Civil War. In times of peace, he entertained the people of New Orleans with his music.

The drum used by Jordan Noble at the Battle of New Orleans in 1815.

THINK ABOUT IT

Slaves were denied military pensions other soldiers received. In 1882, Jordan Noble applied for a pension. He didn't mention he had been a slave during the War of 1812. Do you think that was wrong or right?

$130,000
Starting bid for one of John Noble's drums at an auction in 2016.

- An American soldier bought Jordan Noble.
- Jordan learned to issue commands as an army drummer.
- He helped the Americans win important battles during the War of 1812.

9

4

Anson Stager Stumps the Confederates

During the Civil War, the Union Army relied on the telegraph for communication. Telegraph operators sent messages using Morse code. Dots and dashes indicated letters and numbers. The Confederates knew Morse code, too. They could tap into Union telegraph lines and listen in.

Anson Stager was a Union telegraph operator. Early in the war, he created a way to encrypt important messages. Others helped refine it.

The process started with a code. Operators replaced key words with code words. For instance, "Fort Sumter" became "apple." Frequently used key words had multiple code words. "President" had eight different code words. One was "Bologna."

Operators wrote the message in a set number of columns and rows. They added words to fill the grid. Then they added nonsense words. These would confuse anyone who intercepted the message.

The first word in the message told how to interpret it. It told the receiving operator how many columns and rows the message had. It told him which words to ignore. It also told

Anson Stager in 1859.

CODE VS. CIPHER

Secret messages are sometimes called codes. Sometimes they are called ciphers. What's the difference? In general, a cipher is a set of rules. The rules tell a person how to encode and decode a message. A code replaces specific items with other set items. This requires users to have access to a codebook.

15,000
Miles (24,140 km) of permanent telegraph lines added by the Union during the Civil War.

- Telegraph operator Anson Stager created a Union code for the Civil War.
- Telegraph operators replaced code words with key words when sending important messages.
- The Confederates never broke Stager's code.

him what route was used. One grid had seven columns and 11 rows. The route went up the sixth column, down the third, up the fifth, and so on.

Stager's cipher was a success. The Confederates never cracked it.

A Civil War telegraph and cipher.

5

Dr. Anita McGee Helps Nurses Join the Army

Wars always have casualties. Armies need nurses to care for the sick and wounded. Up through the Civil War, women did most of the nursing. While often paid, they were not part of the military.

After the Civil War, the US Army created the Hospital Corps. Enlisted men joined. After testing and apprenticeship, they became stewards. These hospital stewards were what nurses are today.

In April 1898, the Spanish-American War began. Hundreds of women offered to serve as Army and Navy nurses. The US military believed their Hospital Corps was enough. Others weren't so sure.

Dr. Anita Newcomb McGee graduated from medical school in 1892. She was also a DAR (Daughters of the American Revolution) leader. McGee and the DAR created their own Hospital Corps. This was a group of trained female nurses who were ready to serve the country.

Within months, yellow fever invaded the Army's training camps. The Army and Navy needed more nurses. They asked the DAR and Dr. McGee for help. McGee and the DAR provided

Dr. Anita McGee in 1904.

1,600 nurses. They made sure all had formal training.

The nurses contracted to serve as long as they were needed. They got a salary in return.

Dr. McGee in uniform.

1
Number of women who wore an officer's uniform during the Spanish-American War. (Dr. McGee was the only one.)

- The US Army created a Hospital Corps after the Civil War.
- They still needed women nurses during the Spanish-American War.
- Dr. Anita McGee and the DAR screened nurses for this war.
- Dr. McGee helped create a permanent Nurse Corps for the Army and Navy.

These nurses became the Society of Spanish-American War Nurses. After the war, Dr. McGee ensured the military continued to have trained female nurses. She helped write the bill creating the Army Nurse Corps. President William McKinley signed the bill in February 1901. Seven years later, the Navy created the US Navy Nurse Corps.

Choctaw Soldiers Turn the Tables in World War I

During war, communication is key. Allies need to coordinate their plans. Enemies want to know what those plans are.

In World War I, the Germans had the advantage. They tapped into telephone wires. They received all radio signals. The Germans broke every code the Allies used. Messengers weren't working, either. The Germans killed one of every four. The Allies tried color-coded rockets, carrier pigeons, and buzzers. They were too limited, too slow, and too unreliable.

American troops faced the Germans on the Western Front in fall 1918. They needed to keep the Germans from hearing their plans. One day, a captain heard Choctaw soldiers talking. They weren't speaking English. He stopped and asked what language it was. The soldiers thought they were in trouble. At home in America, Choctaw students were beaten for speaking their native language.

The captain found they had a group of Choctaw speakers. Within hours,

Choctaw soldiers in 1918.

eight had been relocated. Each field headquarters had one.

On October 26, 1918, the Choctaw speakers were put to the test. They relayed an order to move two companies to a new location. The Germans seemed unaware of the move. On October 27, the code talkers organized an assault on the Germans. The attack surprised the Germans.

The Choctaw "code" was a success. So was the attack. Within 72 hours of the first Choctaw transmission, the Germans were retreating. The war ended on November 11, 1918.

2008
The year the Choctaw code talkers were recognized for their contribution to World War I.

- During World War I, the Germans intercepted most Allied messages.
- Germans could not understand the Choctaw language.
- Choctaw code talkers helped the Allies surprise the Germans.

THINK ABOUT IT

The Choctaw soldiers were not American citizens. Native Americans were not given citizenship until 1924. Do you think military service should be rewarded with citizenship?

7

The "Limping Lady" Takes on the Nazis

Virginia Hall grew up in Baltimore, Maryland. She attended college in New York, Paris, and Vienna. She spoke English, French, German, and Italian.

Hall wanted to be a Foreign Service Officer. She couldn't. Women could only be clerks. Hall couldn't do that, either. She had a prosthetic leg. The Foreign Service rejected workers with missing limbs.

When World War II broke out, Hall was in Paris. She volunteered as an ambulance driver for the French army. When France surrendered in May 1940, Hall went to London.

The British Special Operations Executive (SOE) recruited and trained Hall. She returned to France in August 1941. For 14 months, she posed as a *New York Post* newspaper reporter. She was actually working with the resistance. Hall helped downed pilots get home. She got supplies for resistance newspapers and forgers. She acted as a courier for other agents. In November 1942, the Germans put Hall on a wanted poster. She had to leave France.

3
Battalions of French Resistance forces organized, armed, and trained by Hall.

- Virginia Hall couldn't join the American Foreign Service because she had a prosthetic leg.
- During World War II, Hall worked as a spy.
- She led many resistance efforts.

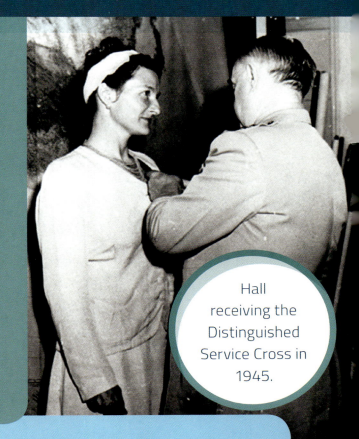

Hall receiving the Distinguished Service Cross in 1945.

CUTHBERT CAUSES TROUBLE

Hall's journey over the Pyrenees was difficult. At one point, she got a message to SOE headquarters in London. She said she was fine, but "Cuthbert" was giving her trouble. Hall was told to eliminate Cuthbert. This was a problem. Cuthbert was Hall's nickname for her prosthetic leg.

Hall hiked over the snowy Pyrenees mountains to Spain. A year later, Hall returned to France disguised as an old peasant. She operated the radio and ran operations. Her team blew up bridges. They derailed German freight trains. They took down telephone lines. They killed or captured hundreds of German soldiers.

Tootsie Rolls Save Marines in Korean War

In late November 1950, United Nations troops tried to push North Korean forces into Manchuria. On the west side of the Chosin Reservoir were 25,000 American Marines. A smaller Army division was on the east. Late at night on November 27, 120,000 Chinese forces attacked. The Marines were outnumbered four to one. The Army, eight to one.

Both divisions fought hard, but conditions were bleak. The air was bitterly cold. Daytime high temperatures were below zero degrees Fahrenheit (-17°C). Nighttime temperatures froze blood. The soldiers were surrounded. Their trucks were pitted with holes. Supplies were running low.

When the Marines ran low on mortar shells, they got on the radio. They requested more "Tootsie Rolls." This was the code name for the shells. A few hours later, planes dropped loads of supplies. The Marines opened

Marines making their way to safety from Chosin Reservoir in December, 1950.

them. They were filled with Tootsie Roll candies.

The Marines improvised. They ate the Tootsie Rolls for energy. They sucked on Tootsie Rolls to soften them up. They molded the candy to plug holes in gas tanks and radiators.

A crippled Army division made it to the Marines' location. Together, they managed to break through the Chinese and make it to safety.

60
Diameter of the mortar shells code-named "Tootsie Rolls" in mm (2.4 in).

- Soldiers were surrounded by enemy troops at the Chosin Reservoir in North Korea.
- They requested more "Tootsie Rolls," the code name for their ammunition.
- They received Tootsie Roll candies instead of mortar shells.
- The candy helped the soldiers escape.

AGAINST ALL ODDS

After the battle, the Army's 7th Division were called cowards. But historians now believe they saved the Marines. The 2,500 Army soldiers kept 20,000 Chinese troops engaged and away from the Marines. 1,500 Army soldiers lost their lives. Many died in hand-to-hand combat. Those that survived did so against all odds.

9
Lucki Allen Paves the Way for Women Interrogators

9
Number of women intelligence officers in the Vietnam War, including Doris Allen.

- Doris Allen served in the Women's Army Corps (WAC), the female branch of the Army.
- Superiors ignored her warning of the Tet Offensive.
- This is considered one of the biggest intelligence failures in Vietnam.

Doris "Lucki" Allen (left) with another member of the WAC.

Doris "Lucki" Allen graduated from the Tuskegee Institute. A physical education major, she started teaching. She played trumpet in a band. After a while, she wanted something more. Allen joined the Army. As a woman, that meant joining the Women's Army Corps (WAC).

Allen served in Japan during the Korean War. Her college degree earned her the position of newspaper editor. After the war,

Map of the 1968 Tet Offensive.

she went to French language school. She also got POW (Prisoner of War) interrogation training. She was the first woman to do so.

During the Vietnam War, Allen worked in Army intelligence. She paid attention to all kinds of enemy communication. She tried to figure out what they meant. She concluded the enemy was planning a major attack for January 3, 1968. When she wrote a report about it, her supervisors ignored it. They didn't believe a WAC could predict such a big, complicated event.

On January 30, 1968, the VC attacked many locations at once. Although the Americans quickly stopped the attack, thousands of lives were lost. This was the Tet Offensive. The Vietnamese name for their Lunar New Year is Tet. That's when the attack happened.

In the years that followed, Allen warned of other threats. Her superiors treated her reports with skepticism. But they checked them out. On at least two incidents, Allen's warnings saved many lives. In 1970, Allen started finding her name on enemy documents. They wanted her eliminated. She returned to the United States.

10
Marine Mammals Perform Important Tasks in Wartime

6

Number of dolphins that patrolled the harbor in Bahrain during the Persian Gulf War.

- The Navy started studying marine mammals in 1959.
- The Marine Mammal Program trains dolphins and sea lions.
- The animals help with surveillance and retrieval efforts.

A bottlenose dolphin in training.

Dolphins and beluga whales can swim fast and dive deep. They can find things quickly underwater. The Navy wanted these abilities in their equipment. In 1959, they started studying the animals.

SEA LION VS. ROBOT

The Navy wants robots to replace their sea lion fleet. In September 2017, sea lions faced off against an underwater glider. The sea lions found the silent robot within minutes. It quickly attached a beacon to the glider. Maybe the robot will have better luck next time.

The Navy discovered the animals were easily trained. They could perform many useful tasks. The Navy's Marine Mammal Program expanded. Two animals performed best: bottlenose dolphins and sea lions.

Dolphins have powerful sonar. They detect objects based on how sound echoes off them. The Navy uses dolphins to locate mines. Dolphins succeed where electronic sonar often fails. This includes noisy harbors, rough sea floors, and among lots of marine plants.

Sea lions have excellent hearing above and below the water. They can accurately tell where sounds are coming from. Sea lions also have great eyesight. They can see in low light and murky water. They excel at finding things that are out of place. Sea lions are often used to find lost equipment.

Sea lions are also good at finding human swimmers. They often patrol submarine bases and other harborside locations. If they detect an intruding swimmer, they attach a cuff with a line to the swimmer's leg. Their human partners hoist the swimmer out of the water.

Marine mammals were deployed to Vietnam and the Persian Gulf. They have worked in various locations around the United States.

11 First American Woman Leads Troops in Combat

Most Americans don't remember Operation Just Cause. On December 20, 1989, American troops invaded Panama. Panama had elected Guillermo Endara president. Dictator Manuel Noriega took control instead. Noriega was backed by Panamanian Defense Forces (PDF).

American combat forces led the invasion. Military Police (MP) forces followed.

Captain Linda Bray led a group of 30 MPs. They were tasked with securing a dog kennel. The MPs expected to find guard dogs. Instead, they faced 40 heavily armed PDF soldiers. The Panamanians refused to leave without a fight.

Bray crashed her jeep through the kennel gate. She commanded her troops. The firefight lasted for hours. The MPs killed three PDF soldiers. They captured one more. The remaining PDF soldiers fled. No Americans were hurt or killed.

The MPs searched the kennel. They found 40 military cots. They

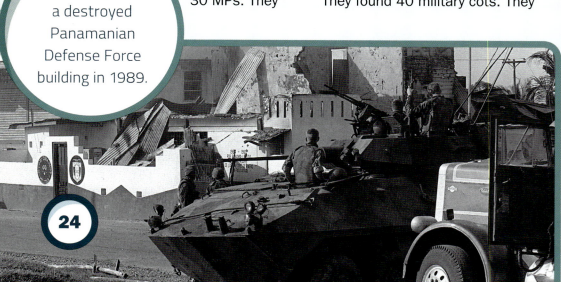

Marines guard a destroyed Panamanian Defense Force building in 1989.

Captain Linda Bray in 1990.

26,000
American troops deployed to Panama in Operation Just Cause.

- Americans invaded Panama in 1989 to help the elected President.
- An MP force went to secure a dog kennel.
- Enemy forces started a firefight.
- The MPs were led by Captain Linda Bray, the first American woman to lead in combat.

found assault rifles, grenades, and thousands of rounds of ammunition. Cuban money and spare uniforms clued them in. The kennel was a PDF special forces barracks.

At first, Captain Bray was congratulated for her success. Then she was accused of wrongdoing. Her superiors questioned how she ended up in combat. Some claimed she made up the story of the firefight. Americans didn't want women in combat.

Captain Bray and others like her did what they had to. Things were unpredictable. Sometimes they had to fight.

THINK ABOUT IT

Hundreds of women found themselves in combat in Panama. None were allowed to wear the Combat Infantry Badge. This badge indicates the soldier has been in combat. Do you think this is right?

12

Soldiers Use Silly String to Detect Trip Wires in Iraq

Disarmed IEDs in eastern Baghdad, 2005.

In May 2003, soldiers in Iraq faced a new threat. A vehicle exploded, killing a soldier from Missouri. It was caused by a new type of bomb, an improvised explosive device (IED).

An IED is made from whatever is available. It might cost a few hundred dollars. It can take out a multi-million-dollar vehicle in one boom. IEDs can be anywhere. They may be buried under a road. They may be planted in a vehicle. They may be hidden in a building. Trip wires make them even more dangerous. Just walking in a room can set one off.

Soldiers found a creative way to detect IED trip wires. Silly String is a thin, light, putty-like string. Soldiers would shoot it into a room. String hanging in the air indicated a trip wire. The string didn't trigger the bombs.

Silly String became a common request from soldiers in Iraq. In 2006, Marcelle Shriver's deployed son requested some. The New Jersey mom sent a few cans. Then she collected more. By December, she had 1,000 cans. Getting them to Iraq proved more difficult.

Silly String comes in aerosol cans. This is considered a hazardous material. By law, only certain companies can ship it. Mrs. Shriver sent a large shipment early in 2007. It took about eight months to get another shipment there. In total, she sent about 100,000 cans.

The US military continues to study IEDs. They developed equipment to detect and defuse them. They've added special armor to their vehicles. They've improved treatments for IED blast victims.

400
Minimum amount of Silly String in the can, in feet (122 m).

- Soldiers in Iraq were not prepared for improvised explosive devices (IEDs).
- Silly String helped detect trip wires.
- One mom provided about 100,000 cans of Silly String to soldiers in Iraq.

Marcella Shriver readies a shipment of Silly String in 2006.

Fact Sheet

- The United States of America declared its independence from Great Britain in 1775. The Revolutionary War ended in 1783. Conflict between England and America continued after the war. The two countries fought again in the War of 1812. That war is often considered the second war of independence.

- The Civil War pitted America's northern states against its southern states. Officers from both sides had trained at West Point. This meant they were familiar with similar tactics and signaling systems.

- Armies have to care for their sick and wounded. This becomes critical during wartime. Nurses didn't have any attachment to the army until the Spanish-American War. Shortly after that war, the Army and Navy created a permanent place for nurses in their ranks.

In 1877, Henry Flipper, a former slave, was the first black person to graduate from West Point.

US soldiers distribute school supplies to children outside Baghdad, Iraq, in 2009.

- World War I and World War II involved many countries around the world. Communication was critical. Each side tried to hide their communications from their enemies. They also tried to get more information about their enemies. By the end of World War II, many nations had organizations dedicated to spying on their enemies.

- The Korean War is often considered a forgotten war. The United States was part of a United Nations force. They were trying to repel Communist forces that wanted to take over South Korea. The Vietnam War was also a fight against Communism.

- After the Vietnam War, the United States engaged in many military operations that are largely forgotten. This includes invasions in Grenada and Panama. It also includes operations in Somalia and Bosnia.

Glossary

barracks
A building or group of buildings where soldiers live.

casualties
People who are hurt, killed, or otherwise lost in battle.

courier
Someone who carries messages, packages, or other objects from one place to another.

deploy
To move soldiers or equipment to where they can be used.

encrypt
To change a message to hide its meaning.

feebleminded
Having a low level of intelligence.

legend
A story from the past that people can't prove to be true or untrue.

prosthetic
An artificial body part.

reveille
An early-morning signal given on a musical instrument to wake up soldiers or call them to duty.

skepticism
Doubting the truth of something.

surveillance
Keeping watch over a person or place.

Tories
American colonists who stayed loyal to the British crown during the American Revolution.

treadle
A foot pedal that powers machines like spinning wheels and lathes.

For More Information

Books

Casey, Susan. *Women Heroes of the American Revolution: 20 Stories of Espionage, Sabotage, Defiance, and Rescue.* Chicago, IL: Chicago Review Press, 2017.

Burgan, Michael. *World War II Spies: An Interactive History Adventure.* North Mankato, MN: Capstone Press, 2013.

Smithsonian Institution. *The Vietnam War: The Definitive Illustrated History.* New York: DK, 2017.

Visit 12StoryLibrary.com

Scan the code or use your school's login at **12StoryLibrary.com** for recent updates about this topic and a full digital version of this book. Enjoy free access to:

- Digital ebook
- Breaking news updates
- Live content feeds
- Videos, interactive maps, and graphics
- Additional web resources

Note to educators: Visit 12StoryLibrary.com/register to sign up for free premium website access. Enjoy live content plus a full digital version of every 12-Story Library book you own for every student at your school.

Index

Allen, Doris, 20-21
American Revolution, 4, 6, 12, 28, 30-31

Bray, Linda, 24-25
Bushnell's Turtle, 4-5

Choctaw language, 14-15
Civil War, 9, 10-11, 12-13, 28
code talkers, 15

drummers, 8-9

Foreign Service, 16-17

Hall, Virginia, 16-17
Hart, Nancy, 6-7

improvised explosive device (IED), 26-27
intelligence officers, 20
Iraq, 26-27, 29

Korean War, 18-19, 20, 29

Marine Mammal Program, 22-23
Marines, 18-19, 24
McGee, Anita, 12-13
Morse code, 10

Noble, Jordan, 8-9
nurses, 12-13, 28

Panama, 24-25, 29
Persian Gulf War, 22

secret messages, 11
Spanish-American War, 12-13, 28
Stager, Anson, 10-11
submarine, 4-5, 23
surveillance, 22, 30

trip wires, 26-27

Vietnam War, 20-21, 29, 31

War of 1812, 8-9, 28
Women in combat, 24-25
Women's Army Corps (WAC), 20
World War I, 14-15, 29
World War II, 16-17, 29, 31

About the Author
Janet Slingerland was an engineer before she started writing books. She lives in New Jersey with her husband, three children, and a dog.

READ MORE FROM 12-STORY LIBRARY

Every 12-Story Library Book is available in many fomats. For more information, visit 12StoryLibrary.com